The Beothuk of Newfoundland

A VANISHED PEOPLE

Ingeborg Marshall

BREAKWATER

Layout/Design: Angela King-Harris

Also by Ingeborg Marshall:
    The Red Ochre People (Douglas & McIntyre, 1977)
    Reports and Letters by George Christopher Pulling
        Relating to the Beothuk Indians of Newfoundland
        (Breakwater, 1989)

The Publisher acknowledges the support of the Canada Council which has helped make this book possible.

The Publisher acknowledges the financial contribution of the Cultural Affairs Division of the Department of Culture, Recreation and Youth, Government of Newfoundland and Labrador, which has helped make this publication possible.

Canadian Cataloguing in Publication Data

Marshall, Ingeborg, 1929-
    The Beothuk of Newfoundland
    ISBN 0-920911-18-8
1. Beothuk Indians - Juvenile literature. 2. Indians
of North America - Newfoundland - Juvenile literature. Title.

E99.B4M37 1989   J971.8'00497   C89-098547-2

Acknowledgements

Shanawdithit's sketches, pages 16, 22, 23, 24, 27, 28, 33, 41, 42 and 43, were reproduced from J.P. Howley, *The Beothuck or Red Indians* (Cambridge: 1915).

The Publisher greatefully acknowledges the following for permission to reproduce photographs from their collections.

The British Museum: 29, 31

Canadian Museum of Civilization, Archaeology Survey of Canada: 32

National Archives of Canada
    Map Division: 22
    Picture Division: title page

National Maritime Museum: 13

Newfoundland Museum: 4, 20, 44, 45

Drawings/Paintings

Angela King-Harris: 7

Gerald Squires: cover, 9, 12, 15, 17, 29 (top left), 37, 40.

Ruth Holmes Whitehead: 31 (right)

Photographs

Dennis Minty: 10, 11, 38, 39. Artifacts are from the collection of the Newfoundland Museum.

The Publisher gratefully acknowledges the generous assistance of Jane Sproull-Thomson, Chief Curator of the Newfoundland Museum, in providing access to the Museum's collection and permitting reproduction of the photographs.

The Publisher gratefully acknowledges the cooperation of Douglas & McIntyre, Publishers.

Contents

1 *The People and the Land*

The Beothuk lived on the island of Newfoundland for many centuries until the last of them died over 150 years ago. Today, some of the older people in communities to the north still tell stories about the Beothuk, and fishermen occasionally come upon their tools on beaches or in caves. Archaeologists, searching for clues to the past, discover Beothuk camp sites and burials. These traces and stories, supplemented by records from settlers, explorers, and Beothuk captives, are all we have left of the Beothuk Indians.

The Beothuk Indians were tall, strong people with dark eyes and long, black hair which they sometimes wore braided and decorated with feathers. They dressed in animal skins, hunted with bows and arrows, and covered their bodies, clothes and weapons with a mixture of red ochre and oil. This mixture protected their skin against the cold in winter and insects in summer. The Beothuk also believed that the ochre had life-giving power. To the Europeans who came to the island, the Beothuk, with their red, covered skins, must have looked strange, even frightening. The Europeans called them 'Red Indians'.

The Indians called themselves *Beothuk* which means 'people' in their language. Experts on language, called linguists, have studied Beothuk words. They think that their language is related to an earlier form of the Algonkian language and may have separated from it one or two thousand years ago.

The ancestors of the Newfoundland Beothuk originally lived in Labrador. Archaeologists believe they first came to Newfoundland about 2000 years ago and may have moved back and forth to Labrador for several centuries. The Strait of Belle Isle, separating the island of Newfoundland from Labrador, is only 18 kilometres wide at one point and could be crossed by canoe in summer or on foot over the ice in winter. Later, the Indians no longer left Newfoundland and it was here that they developed the culture which we recognize as Beothuk, though they were still part of the Algonkian family of tribes.

Remains of Beothuk camps and burials have been found on the coast of the Avalon Peninsula, on the southern and western shore of the island and most often on beaches or islands in Bonavista and Notre Dame Bays. The best known inland hunting ground of the Beothuk was the country around the Exploits River and Red Indian Lake.

The natural resources of Newfoundland were well suited to support hunting and fishing people like the Beothuk. Thousands of caribou grazed in the barrens and woodlands. Bear, beaver, wolf, lynx, fox and smaller mammals inhabited the fir and spruce forests from coast to coast. Brooks and rivers were filled with salmon and trout, and migratory geese and ducks came to breed on the many lakes. The sea provided fish, shellfish and other seafood as well as seals, walrus and whales; sea birds were also plentiful. The island's subarctic summers were warm but short, and the long winters were cold and stormy with much snowfall. The Indians knew how to survive well in this climate, and knew how to find food in every season.

The Beothuk Indians were not the first people to live on the island of Newfoundland. About 5000 years before present (meaning before 1950 and usually referred to as B.P.), an ancient race of people we call the Maritime Archaic Indians lived on the shores of Newfoundland. They stayed for 2000 years, until about 3000 B.P. To this day, some of their burial places as well as large, polished stone tools are found from time to time near the coast. Archaeologists believe that the Beothuk may have been related to these early people because they had some of the same customs: for example, they both carved bone pendants and both included red ochre in their burials as well as parts of animals, such as birds' feet and beaks, tools, weapons and other items of daily use.

Another group of people who lived on the coasts of this island were Paleo Eskimos. 'Paleo' means ancient. These Eskimos came to Newfoundland from the far north about 3000 B.P. They were followed by more and more Eskimos, some of them from Cape Dorset, so we call them Dorset Eskimos. The Eskimos stayed in Newfoundland for nearly 2000 years, about as long as the Maritime Archaic Indians before them.

Dorset Eskimos may have met the ancestors of the Beothuk, and may have traded tools with them or fought against them. But over time the Eskimo population became smaller and smaller and, by 1000 B.P., no Eskimos were left in Newfoundland. The Beothuk became the only people living on the island.

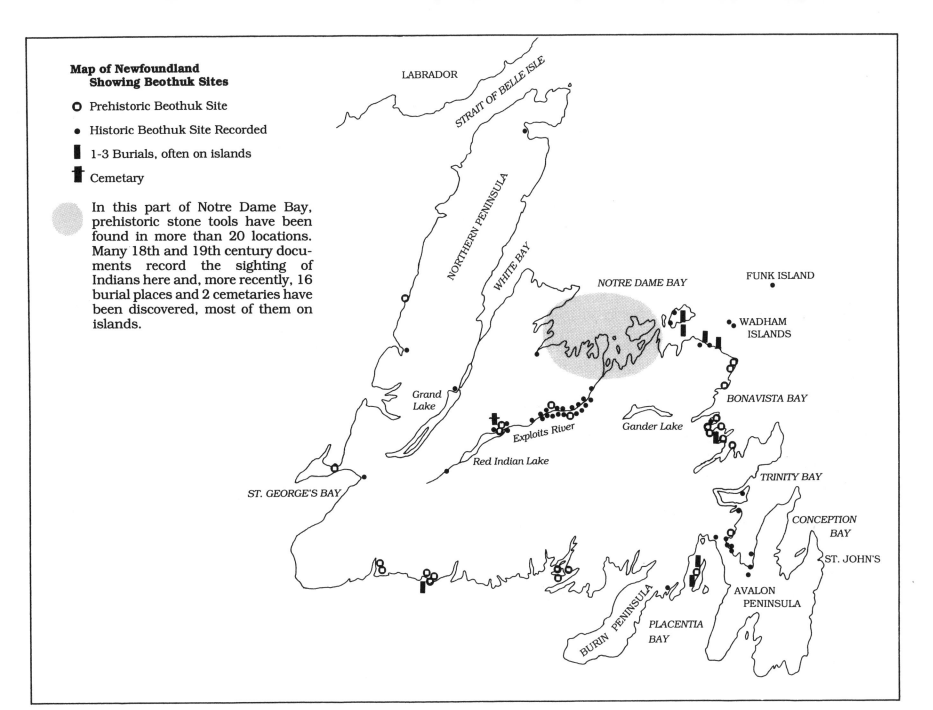

Map of Newfoundland Showing Beothuk Sites

O Prehistoric Beothuk Site

● Historic Beothuk Site Recorded

▮ 1-3 Burials, often on islands

♱ Cemetary

In this part of Notre Dame Bay, prehistoric stone tools have been found in more than 20 locations. Many 18th and 19th century documents record the sighting of Indians here and, more recently, 16 burial places and 2 cemetaries have been discovered, most of them on islands.

LABRADOR

STRAIT OF BELLE ISLE

NORTHERN PENINSULA

WHITE BAY

NOTRE DAME BAY

FUNK ISLAND

WADHAM ISLANDS

Grand Lake

BONAVISTA BAY

Exploits River

Gander Lake

Red Indian Lake

TRINITY BAY

ST. GEORGE'S BAY

CONCEPTION BAY

ST. JOHN'S

AVALON PENINSULA

BURIN PENINSULA

PLACENTIA BAY

2 Transportation

We are not sure how the Beothuk reached Newfoundland. They could have walked over the Strait of Belle Isle when the sea was frozen in winter or paddled across in their canoes in summer. Canoeing in the sea is dangerous, but the Beothuk canoes were seaworthy and different in design from other Indian canoes. Seaworthy canoes were important for the Beothuk because they hunted and fished in the ocean and often buried their dead on islands. They even went 60 kilometres out into the Atlantic to the Funk Islands where they hunted and collected eggs of the Great Auk, a large flightless bird that is now extinct. A trip of this distance was a very daring voyage by canoe!

Today, the drawings and descriptions of Beothuk canoes left by early settlers and explorers tell us what some of them looked like. A miniature copy of a Beothuk canoe was also recently discovered in the Maritime Museum in London. It was made by Shanawdithit, a Beothuk woman, who was captured and lived with a settler family on Exploits Island for several years.

Beothuk canoes were between 3.5 and 6.5 metres long and could carry up to 8 or 10 adults. Their special features were a high-curved front and back to protect the occupants from spray, and sides that rose high in the middle so that water would not pour into the craft when it tipped sideways. While most bark canoes of other Indians had a flat or rounded bottom from which the sides rose up gently, the sides on Beothuk canoes flared straight out from the central timber or keelson; seen from the front, Beothuk canoes looked pointed at the bottom. This feature gave the canoes great depth and prevented them from being blown off course.

To build a canoe, the Beothuk stripped sheets of birch bark from large trees and sewed them together to form a single sheet. It was laid out on the ground with the smooth inner bark facing down. This smooth surface became the outside of the canoe. A piece of spruce the length of the canoe was placed in the centre of the bark sheet to serve as a keelson or frame. The bark was then folded upwards along the keelson to form the sides and was held up by stakes driven into the ground.

Now the canoe was ready to be strengthened. The upper edges of the sides were fortified with long, tapered poles of spruce, called gunwales, that were

This stone knife was excavated by archaeologists from a Beothuk campsite. It was originally tied to a wooden handle.

(Overleaf) The Beothuk hunted sea birds from their canoes.

A bone harpoon head with an iron point. The two forked ends fitted onto the end of a long wooden shaft or handle. The harpoon head has a hole for attaching a line.

(Above Left) Two moccasins from a boy's grave. The moccasins had been rubbed with a mixture of grease and red ochre. (Left) A necklace of carved bone pieces and an animal tooth. It may have belonged to a shaman, a person with special knowledge about the spirit world. The carvings could have represented his animal helpers. (Above) The miniature birch bark canoe very clearly shows the unique shape of Beothuk canoes, with high pointed ends and rising sides. The canoe was found in a grave.

(Overleaf) A depiction of a Beothuk caribou hunt.

11

This head-on view of a Beothuk canoe shows the sharp fold of the bark cover over the keelson and the straight flaring sides that made the Beothuk canoe so different from other Indian canoes.

lashed to the bark. At both ends of the canoe, the bark cover was cut to its proper shape and sewn together. All lashing and sewing was done with split spruce roots. Since the women were the most skilled at sewing, they usually completed this part of the job. When all the sewing was done, the two sides of the canoe were sprung open like a purse.

The next step was to place crossbars or 'thwarts' at the middle and at each end, to hold the sides apart. Inside, the birch bark was protected with wooden slats laid lengthwise. Curved sticks known as ribs were placed over them to hold the slats and keelson in place. The rib ends were tucked under the gunwales. The seams and any thin patches in the bark were waterproofed with a thick coating of heated tree gum, charcoal, and red ochre. When the coating had cooled and dried, the canoe could be launched.

Shanawdithit made this 54 cm long canoe model from birch bark while living on Exploits Island. She gave it to Captain W.H. Jones of HMS Orestes in 1826 or 1827.

Because Beothuk canoes were very light and had no flat bottom to rest on, they would not stay upright in the water without ballast. Rocks, covered with moss and sods to make them more comfortable to kneel on, were often used for ballast. How tippy could a canoe with a pointed bottom be? To find out, Scott James from Grand Falls built one from plywood. He found it took time and patience to ballast it with rocks but, once this was accomplished, the canoe was very stable and easily cut through the waves.

Canoes were the most important means of transportation inland as well as at sea. The Beothuk had no horses or dogs to help them carry their loads, and it was difficult to push through the heavy undergrowth in the forests or to cross the spongy marshes. The easiest and quickest way to travel was by canoe along the chains of ponds and rivers, carrying the craft around rapids or across land barriers. Since bark canoes were light, a strong person could lift a small one with one hand or carry it on his shoulders for a good distance.

Winter called for different means of transportation. As soon as the snow covered the ground, the Indians used sleds to transport their belongings and to bring meat from the storehouses to their *mamateeks*, or houses. Snowshoes were used for walking over deep snow. The frame of a snowshoe was made by bending a strip of flexible wood into a loop, then tying the ends together to form a tail in the back. A crossbar was lashed to the frame, and the open spaces were webbed with wet seal or caribou hide strips. These skin strips became tight as they dried out.

Tracks of Beothuk snowshoes were a sure sign for English trappers that Indians had been in the area. One trapper measured a snowshoe print and recorded that the webbed part was 70 cm long, and the tail 30 cm long.

Trial run of a plywood replica of a Beothuk canoe in New Bay. The occupants are Scott James, who made the canoe, and the author.

3 Tools and Weapons

Though the Beothuk were different in many ways from the Indians of eastern Canada, they used the same weapons for hunting and fighting, namely bows, arrows and spears. They were excellent archers and could aim and fire their arrows quickly. A hunter held his bow and arrows in his left hand, then passed one arrow at a time to the right hand which set the end of the arrow in the bowstring. He then pulled the string back and shot the arrow off.

Beothuk bows were made from the smooth, seasoned branches of spruce or mountain ash. They were about a metre and a half long and tapered at both ends. Frequent rubbings with red ochre and grease kept them from drying out. For bowstrings, the Beothuk used animal sinews that they twisted and rolled together so that they would be strong and not stretch too much.

A supply of arrows was carried in a quiver which was a birch bark tube open at one end. The arrows were thin, light and hafted with stone, and later metal, arrowheads. The back of each arrow was notched for the bow string and had two strips of feather tied to it for stability. Arrows used for hunting small birds were blunt so that they could kill the bird without piercing it.

Above, a blunt arrow; and below bow and arrows in a birch bark quiver, taken from a drawing by John Cartwright.

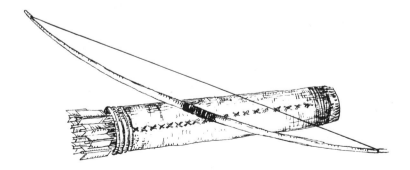

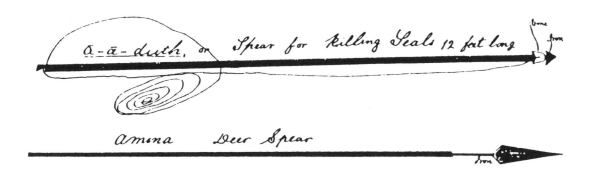

a-ā-duth, or Spear for killing Seals 12 feet long

amina   Deer Spear

A sealing harpoon and a spear used for hunting caribou as drawn by Shanawdithit. The explanations she gave were recorded by Cormack.

Spears with long stone or bone points were used for hunting caribou. After European fishermen came to Newfoundland, the Indians used iron points. The Beothuk often hunted caribou from canoes. They paddled closer and closer to a swimming caribou and when they got as close as they could, one man would drive his spear into the animal. The crew had to be very careful not to tip the canoe.

Hunting seals posed another problem: how to keep the wounded seal from diving under the ice and escaping. The Beothuk solved this problem by using a special sealing harpoon with a barbed head which easily detached from its wooden handle but was tied to a long string of caribou skin. The hunter used the wooden harpoon handle to thrust the sharp point into the seal and the handle was then pulled back leaving the harpoon head stuck in the seal's body. The hunter held on to the string that was attached to the harpoon head and even if the seal dived, it could not get away. An adult seal could pull very hard, so the hunter had to brace himself so as not to be pulled into the water.

When the seal tired out, it was pulled to shore or onto the ice and killed. The harpoon head was cut free to be used again. Harpoons took a long time to make, and a hunter regretted when a seal got away with one.

For tools, the Beothuk made use of the many materials they found around them. A beach rock of the right size and shape made a good hammer. Sharp bones and stones were used for scraping and softening skins. For woodworking the Beothuk made 'crooked' knives by fitting a beaver tooth on a wooden handle. The proper way to use this knife was to pull the tooth blade sideways towards the user. Since beaver teeth were strong enough to cut down trees, they made sharp and long lasting knife blades.

It seems that the Beothuk were not familiar with the bow drill; other Indians used this tool to make holes by turning a pointed stick around and around on an object until it was pierced through. Instead, the Beothuk gouged holes in bone or wood with a sharp stone tool. Leather and bark were pierced with a pointed piece of bone or antler, hafted to a handle; this tool is called an awl.

In prehistoric times different types of knives for cutting bark, meat and skins as well as chopping tools, arrowheads and spear points were made of stone, such as chert or flint. This type of stone could be worked into different shapes by chipping off flakes. A toolmaker knew just how to strike and chip the stone to get the shape he wanted. Working or 'knapping' stone was an important craft that took skill and practice. The finished tool was razor sharp and, when it became blunt, it could be re-chipped to make it sharp again.

With the coming of the Europeans, Beothuk tools changed. The Beothuk obtained iron from the Europeans, often by stealing their tools or traps. They took pieces of iron and heated them in a fire, then beat the pieces on a flat rock to make arrowheads or knife blades. These new tools replaced the stone ones, since iron tools were easier to make and lasted longer. Iron chopping tools or axes were particularly valued in the construction of caribou fences, for which so many trees had to be cut down.

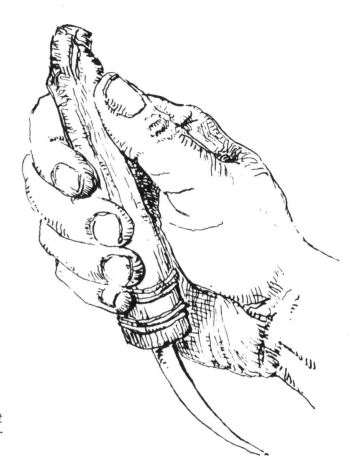

A crooked knife in use. To make one, the Indians would haft a beaver tooth to a curved wooden handle. When shaving or cutting wood, the knife was pulled toward the user.

17

4 Hunting and Warfare

The Beothuk Indians moved from place to place with the seasons. In fall they hunted caribou in the forest and stayed there for the winter; in spring they came to the coast to catch seals, to fish and collect seafood and they remained close to the sea until the end of the summer.

Caribou are migratory animals that move about in herds. In summer they graze on open ground and in fall they travel to more sheltered feeding places. At this time, the caribou are fat and their fur is at its best for clothing. The best time to hunt large numbers of caribou is during their travel. A herd takes much the same route every year, and the animals follow leaders in the herd. Knowing this, the Beothuk drove the leading animals into a fenced area, expecting the rest of the herd to follow. By using this method, they were able to kill many caribou in a few days and thereby obtain plenty of meat for their families to last them through the long winter. The Beothuk called the caribou *osweet.*

To get ready for the caribou drive, families gathered together in early fall at a river or lake where they thought the caribou would cross. Here they built fences along both sides of the shore, leaving only small openings for the animals to come to the water. More fences, starting far back in the woods, guided the caribou straight to the openings. The fences were made by cutting off the upper parts of trees and leaving them hanging on their stumps, so that they formed a kind of triangle with the ground. When the trees piled up, they formed a thicket that the caribou could neither go through nor jump over.

If there were not enough trees for a fence, the Beothuk stuck poles in the ground and tied birch bark tassels to their tops. The tassels flapped in the wind and frightened the caribou. The animals did not dare to pass between the poles, and would only get to the water where gaps had been left for them.

Waiting for the caribou, several Indians would hide in the forest. When a caribou herd came near, the Indians made loud noises to drive the caribou toward the fences. Meanwhile, other Beothuk were ready in their canoes to chase the caribou in the water and kill them with their long spears. This was easier than spearing them on land, since caribou could not swim as fast as the Indians could paddle. Caribou that reached the opposite shore faced more fences and more Indians who shot them before they could escape into the forest.

Since the caribou did not cross a river or lake at exactly the same spot every year, the Beothuk had to build many kilometres of fences to be ready for them at any point. The main hunting ground of the Beothuk along the Exploits River had fences stretching for up to 50 kilometres. Many families had to work together to build the fences and keep them in repair; they shared the work and afterwards shared the meat and skins.

The caribou drive marked the approach of winter with low temperatures and heavy snowfalls. During the winter, food gathering was limited to trapping small mammals and catching birds. 'Ptarmigan' or partridge, a favorite game bird in Newfoundland, move slowly in cold weather; a skilled hunter can catch a whole flock by knocking the birds— one by one— from the branches on which they roost.

When spring came, the Beothuk left their winter camps and went in small groups to the coast. Here they hunted harp seals that came into the bays and close to shore. They chased the seals in the water with canoes and harpooned them, or clubbed them on the ice.

A little later in the year, whales too came into the coastal waters. They were highly prized by the Indians, because a single large whale could feed a family for weeks! We know little about the methods that the Beothuk used to catch whales. They probably pursued them in their canoes as did other Indian tribes; or maybe they drove 'pods' or groups of small whales into the shallows of a bay where they could kill them with clubs and axes. Even today, whales sometimes get stranded in shallow water and are taken by fishermen.

In early summer, the Beothuk caught salmon which came into many rivers to spawn upstream. They may have blocked river mouths with stone weirs and speared the salmon as they got caught in the enclosure. Sea birds such as murre, puffins and guillemot were hunted with bow and arrow. The Indians shot at them from hiding places near the rock cliffs where the birds perched, or they took them by surprise in their nesting colonies.

As summer changed to fall, the families moved inland again to the rivers and lakes to hunt caribou. They hunted other mammals too; beaver, marten, fox and otter were valued for both their meat and fur. The Beothuk also pursued the powerful black bear; imagine the courage it would have taken to attack a grown bear with only a bow and arrow!

The Beothuk used their bows and arrows not only for hunting but also in fights with other peoples. They protected themselves with round pinewood shields. Rather than fighting open battles, the Beothuk would often make hit-and-run attacks on small groups of enemies in their camps or while they were travelling. The Inuit, who came in their *umiaks* from Labrador, were said to be powerful and skilled fighters. They often won against the Beothuk. But among the Micmacs, the Beothuk were said to be impossible to beat. It is said that only when the Micmacs got guns were they able to defeat the Beothuk.

In attacks on English fishermen or settlers the Beothuk usually shot arrows from an ambush. They could trick the fishermen by first letting the arrows fall short of their targets. The fishermen were thereby led to believe that the Indians could not shoot very far. But when they came close to the Indians' hiding place, the Beothuk showered them with arrows and ducked behind rocks to avoid their gun shots. In these skirmishes the Beothuk did not use their wooden shields since shot would go right through them.

To signify peace, a Beothuk man would approach strangers or enemies with a white skin or a green branch. When John Guy, an English settler, met with Beothuk in 1612, one of them shook a white wolf skin and made speeches; then all the Indians leaped, danced and sang to show their friendliness. They gave Guy and his men shell necklaces and arrows without points, then they sat down together to share a meal.

The signal for peace was not always understood. When the Beothuk Demasduwit was captured in 1819, her husband, chief Nonosbawsut, asked for her release by stepping forward with a green branch and making a long speech. Unfortunately, none of the settlers could understand what he said, and thinking he was angry, they killed him.

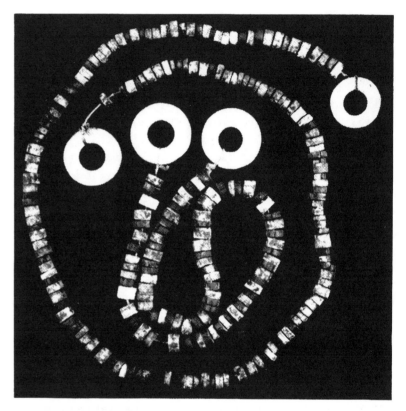

Two strings of flat beads, used as necklaces or counters, found in Beothuk graves. The small beads were made from shell, clay pipe stems and birch bark; the large white rings at either end were made from shells.

5 Mamateeks

The Beothuk word for house is *mamateek*. Summer mamateeks looked very much like the round wigwams of other northeastern Indians. To construct one the Beothuk first dug out a shallow round pit and to this day such pits can be found on old Beothuk campsites. They then tied long poles together at the top and set them on the ground by spreading the lower ends in a circle around the edge of the pit. A couple of small trees were bent into hoops and tied to the inside at different heights to keep the poles in position. Shorter poles were stuck into the ground to fill the gaps, their tops were tied to the hoops. The whole frame was then covered with sheets of birch bark, starting at the bottom and working up in overlapping layers, like tiles. The bark was tied to the frame with spruce roots. Poles, leaning against the bark on the outside, held it in place. A smoke hole was left open at the top. If there was no birch bark to be had, the Beothuk used spruce bark or caribou skins instead.

Every mamateek had a fireplace in the centre. Long, narrow hollows in the ground around it formed sleeping places. For comfort, these hollows were lined with the tender branches of fir, or with grass or skins. In spring and summer, one, two or more families camped together, each in its own mamateek. Because the Indians moved from place to place, they had to build several mamateeks in a season.

Winter mamateeks were usually constructed inland near a river or lake in clusters of up to ten houses, forming a village. They were more solid and better insulated than summer mamateeks to withstand the harsh storms and freezing cold of winter. English settlers and soldiers who saw these houses were surprised by their size and sturdiness. Some Englishmen spent a night in a winter mamateek after the Indians had run away and found that, once a fire was going, the mamateek was comfortably warm.

Winter houses were made in different shapes and sizes. They could be rectangular or five, six or eight sided and large enough for 10 to 20 people. Several families shared a winter mamateek, but each person had a special place in it. The house floor was dug out to a depth of about 20 cm and had a fireplace in the centre with sleeping hollows around it. Walls were made of tree trunks driven upright into the ground. All the cracks were stuffed with moss. The cone-shaped roof was a frame of poles and hoops just like the frame

Summer mameteek illustrated by John Cartwright in 1768. The poles with birch bark tassels tied to them were used in making caribou fences.

of a summer mamateek. The Beothuk covered the roof with three coats of birch bark, placing thick layers of moss and sods between them. The smoke hole at the top was held fast with clay and the entrance was covered with caribou skins.

To make the mamateek warmer, earth was banked up against the outside walls. Inside, the walls were covered with caribou skins and were used to hang up bows, arrows, spears and tools. Food was stored on beams or shelves inside the roof. Since a lot of time would be spent indoors in winter, mamateeks had space for making tools and clothes and for playing games.

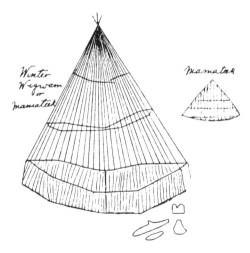

Shanawdithit's drawings of a winter and a summer mamateek. She has sketched the basic structures, including the hoops inside, rather than the finished houses. Perhaps the uprights at the bottom look short because they were partly covered with earth.

6 Social Life

The Beothuk tribe was divided into bands of up to 60 or 80 people. Each band had a chief who was chosen for his good conduct, his hunting skills and his ability to lead the people in times of trouble. As a sign of his special position, a chief had a long, ochre-coloured stave which was topped with a geometrical figure, a whale's tail, a half-moon or a fishing boat. We do not know the exact meaning of these figures; they may have symbolized a particular event or a supernatural power. A chief had little authority over his band; important decisions were made in council with other respected band members. A council would meet to decide whether a war party should be sent off, whether the band should join with others, or where and when to stage a caribou drive or build a winter village.

Among the Beothuk each man had only one wife who was respected as an important partner. Men and women had different work and duties. Men hunted and trapped and fought against enemies. Women cared for the children, looked after the fire and prepared food. Women also made the warm clothes that were needed in winter.

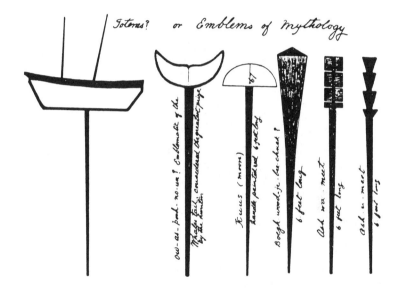

Six-metre-long staves with symbols of Beothuk mythology, as drawn by Shanawdithit. Cormack wrote down the names of the staves, but failed to give a proper explanation of their significance. The first three represent a fishing boat, a whale's tail, and a half moon.

Shanawdithit's drawing of a dancing woman. Her garment is decorated with stitched patterns and is fringed around the lower edges. It is belted at the waist, while the upper part falls in a large fold over the waist and hips.

As they helped with the chores, the children learned the skills of their elders. Girls learned from their mothers how to make a fire and keep it going, how to collect, preserve and cook food, and how to prepare skins and make clothing. Boys were taught how to stalk, hunt and trap animals as well as other skills needed to become successful hunters and warriors. Both boys and girls had to be able to build a mamateek and had to know how to build, repair and handle a canoe.

Old people were looked up to and stayed within the family; they helped to prepare food or make tools and weapons or gave advice when a person was sick. The Beothuk got their medicines, like their food, from the world around them. The Indians knew many plants and roots that cured illnesses or healed wounds. They also used a steam bath for cleansing and for relief from aches and pains. A small tent of branches covered with skins was built over hot rocks. The patient would creep under the skins with a bucket of water and splash the hot rocks to produce steam.

Every spring, each band gathered for an ochering ceremony by a lake or river. During the ceremony, every person applied a fresh coat of the dye to their skin. Babies who were born during the previous year received their first coat of ochre. It was the mark of the tribe. The Beothuk called the red ochre *odemen*.

Shortly after this ceremony, the Indians separated and went off to the coast. One, two or several families hunted and fished together through spring and summer. In early fall the band met again for the caribou drive. Once they had settled down for the winter, the people had time to tell stories and play games.

Although we know little about how the Beothuk entertained themselves they did play a gambling game, called the bowl game, that was a favourite pastime of many Indians. It was played with flat bone pieces that were marked on one side and tossed from a bowl or tray into the air. The aim was to have all the pieces fall on the ground with all the marked sides either up or down. Each player received points according to which way the game pieces fell.

Fall and winter were also the time when councils and ceremonial feasts were held. Feasts in honour of supernatural powers or animal spirits were celebrated according to strict rules and included eating, making speeches, singing, dancing and wearing special clothes. Other special occasions were marriage celebrations and victory feasts. The Beothuk celebrated the killing of an enemy by beheading him and placing the head on a pole around which they sang and danced.

The Beothuk passed on their history, adventures and beliefs in songs; they had songs about the animals they hunted, about their tools and boats, about mountains and water and all the things that were important to them in their daily lives. There were other songs, too, that told of famous deeds, of other tribes, and of the white men. In these songs, the Indians remembered with pride the courage and cunning of their people. One person or a small group would sing their story and sometimes everyone joined in a song.

Myths retold from one generation to the next kept alive the Indians' knowledge of their relationship with the world around them. The Beothuk's story of their origin tells of a cluster of arrows which were stuck in the ground and turned into people. In myth, these people were the Beothuk's ancestors.

7 Food

Since the Beothuk lived from hunting and gathering, they ate the foods of the season. In spring, fresh seal meat was a welcome change in the diet after a long winter of eating stored caribou meat. Seals have a great deal of fat which the Indians melted down into oil and kept in bags made of seal bladders. This oil was used for food, or it was mixed with ochre for rubbing on their bodies and clothes, tools and implements.

The sea offered a rich variety of other foods as well—lobsters, clams, mussels and fish. Every year in June, caplin arrived in the bays and inlets to spawn along the water's edge. They swam so closely packed together that a person wading along the beach could pick them up with his hands.

A favourite food of the Indians was Atlantic salmon. In June salmon head into rivers to lay their eggs in shallow waters upstream. The Indians usually caught salmon in the mouths of rivers, spearing them with great skill. Fresh salmon made delicious meals; dried or smoked, the salmon could be stored for the winter. Sometimes whales came into the bays and were caught or got stranded, and they supplied large amounts of oil and meat.

Sea birds which live on Newfoundland's shores by the thousands were valued by the Beothuk for their meat, eggs and feathered skins. These birds nest in large colonies on rock faces and cliffs. The Beothuk sought out their nesting grounds and collected great numbers of eggs. Eggs were either eaten fresh or preserved in different ways. Sometimes, they were mixed with seal fat, liver, fish and other foods and stuffed into seal intestines to make a kind of sausage. These sausages could be kept for times when fresh food was scarce. Another method of preserving eggs was to boil and dry them and crush the yolks into powder which was nourishing and easy to carry. Eggs were also boiled, mixed with caribou or seal fat and dried in the sun in the shape of small cakes. Since the Beothuk had no grain to make flour for baking, these cakes were their closest food to bread.

When berries ripened in August and September, Beothuk women and children went berry picking as we do, collecting blueberries, partridge berries, marsh berries, raspberries, cranberries, wild currants, bake-apples and others. The Beothuk had no sugar to make jam, so they would have saved the berries for winter by drying them or storing them in oil. They also dug up roots from wild plants, ate herbs and cut the inner bark of spruce trees for food.

In early fall the Beothuk moved back into the forest to get ready for the winter. They hunted beaver and other small mammals for their furs and meat; the fleshy beaver tail was thought to be a great treat! When geese and ducks flocked together on lakes on their way south, the skilled hunters were able to catch plenty of fowl.

As the herds of caribou returned from the barrens and neared the fence traps, the big hunt was on. The Indians were kept busy for weeks, cutting and preserving the meat and skins. During the winter months, they lived mainly on caribou meat from the fall hunt.

The Beothuk had several ways of keeping the meat and fat from spoiling. Caribou fat was melted down and stored in bark dishes. The meat was cut into thin strips, washed and then packed tightly with layers of melted fat into sheets of birch bark. Larger chunks of meat were taken from the bone and tied together in packages weighing up to two hundred pounds. They were wrapped up in birch or spruce bark, with the tongue and heart placed in the centre of the package. As soon as frost set in, the packages of meat were frozen and would then keep all winter. To prevent animals from stealing their food, the Beothuk stowed it in sturdy storehouses. Food was also kept next to the mamateeks in pits that were lined and covered with birch bark.

Another method of preserving meat and fish was to dry or smoke it in smoke houses. These houses were made of poles and had open shelves which let air and smoke circulate freely. Fish or meat treated in this way would keep for many months.

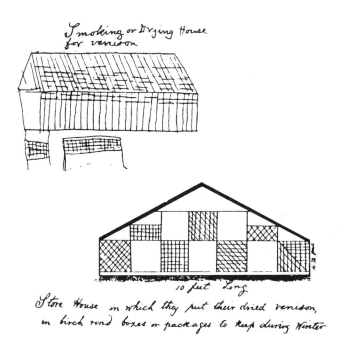

"Smoking or drying house for venison" and "store house in which they put their dried venison in birch rind boxes or packages to keep during winter," drawn by Shanawdithit.

For cooking food, the Beothuk used open fires. A fire was started by striking two pieces of iron pyrite together and catching the sparks with bird down or dry moss. When a good fire was going, they roasted large pieces of meat or whole birds over it on a wooden spit. The larger bones were cracked open because the Indians liked to eat the marrow in the centre. Smaller pieces of meat were pushed onto roasting sticks and placed around the fire to broil. The Indians also made soup from birds, meat or bones in birch bark pots. They heated stones in the fire and dropped them into the soup to bring it to the boiling point. More hot rocks

were added to keep the pot on the boil until the meat was done. Other than soup, the Beothuk drank mostly water.

Birch bark was one of the Beothuk's most important raw materials. The Beothuk called it *paushe*e. It was not only needed for covering canoes and mamateeks, but also for making containers. Pieces of bark were loosened from the tree with great care so the tree would not die. It was then cut into different patterns, folded into dishes, and tightly sewn with roots. The simplest type of dish was folded from a rectangular piece of bark as is shown below. Other containers were fancier. To decorate the dishes, the Beothuk stitched patterns with split root strands and cut the edges with a sawtooth pattern. Small ones were used for cups; others were as large as buckets and served as containers or cooking pots. Some English sailors who surprised a group of Beothuk while they were feasting said that they had three large bark pots, each holding twelve birds the size of ducks!

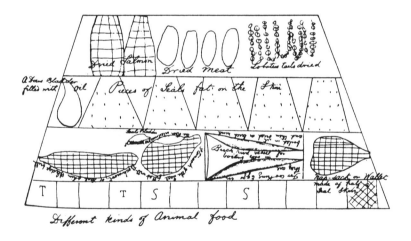

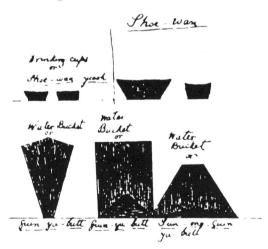

Two sketches by Shanawdithit: The one above shows a display of food with dried salmon, meat and lobster tails, seal oil in seal and caribou bladders, seal fat left on the skin, boiled and dried eggs in bark containers, and a seal stomach filled with intestines. The drawing on the right shows birch bark containers of different sizes: small drinking cups, household dishes, and three types of water buckets.

This is how a simple birch bark dish was folded from a rectangular piece of bark.

An oval meat dish (left), 47cm long and 18cm high, with loops for a carrying cord. Note the root-stitch decorations. Above is a plain mug-shaped container with sawtooth edges. Both dish and container were rubbed with red ochre. The containers come from Nonosbawsut's burial hut at Red Indian Lake.

8 Clothing

To protect themselves against the icy Newfoundland winters, the Beothuk needed warm clothing. Their clothes were mainly made of caribou hide. The winter fur of the caribou is thick and light, and to get the most warmth from it the Beothuk wore the fur side against their bodies. Other garments were made from caribou leather that was tanned on both sides or from beaver, seal, fox or otter furs or even from feathered bird skins. The outside of the garments was covered with a mixture of grease and ochre to keep it soft and make it waterproof. The Beothuk also believed that the red ochre would protect them from harmful spirits.

Preparing the skins and making clothes was usually the work of women. A fresh skin was scraped to get rid of all traces of flesh and fat. Then it was cured by rubbing the flesh side with animal brain or other tanning agents. The skin was stretched for drying on a wooden frame and made pliable by rubbing the leather side with a stone or bone tool. When the skins were dry, the edges were softened by chewing the leather to make sewing easier. Sewing meant pushing holes in the skin with an awl, then threading a length of sinew through. Since sewing was such a laborious job, clothing had as few seams as possible.

For their main robe, which they wore thrown over the shoulders, the Beothuk sewed two caribou hides together. The ends were crossed over the chest like a shawl, and the robe or mantle was belted at the waist. It was trimmed around the neck and front with beaver and otter fur. At the back, the trim formed a wide collar that could be pulled over the head in bad weather. Women's robes also had hoods for carrying babies.

The robe or mantle reached down to the knees and covered the arms as far as the elbow, keeping the arms from moving freely. When a man wanted to use his bow or spear, he slipped one shoulder out of his robe; the belt kept it from falling down. In the summer and fall, the Beothuk wore only a loin cloth, a small skin hung in front from a belt. Going without the heavy mantle made it much easier to chase game.

There were many ways of decorating the robes. Some had fringes along the bottom edges, perhaps with shells, beads, animal teeth, claws or feathers tied to them. Others had stitched patterns on them, made by laying bird quills or rolled up intestines on the leather and sewing them over with sinew. This produced an interesting ribbed effect. Ornaments and decorations not only made the clothes look more attractive, but may also have been used to give magic protection.

In winter the Beothuk wore leggings or skin pants and arm coverings of caribou skin to keep them warm. They also had moccasins and mittens. Moccasins found in the burial of a young boy looked different from those of other Indians as they were box shaped at the toe and had pointed heels. Some were high like ankle boots and others had fringes around the upper edges. Dressed in a robe of caribou fur with a wide collar or hood and with pants, boots, arm coverings and mittens, a Beothuk was well protected in cold and stormy weather.

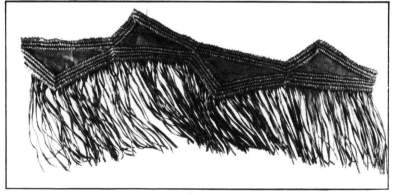

Part of a piece of decorated clothing. The leather fringes hang from a piece of leather that is divided into triangles. These triangles are outlined by ribbed stitching. The piece was removed by Cormack from Nonosbawsut's burial hut at Red Indian Lake.

These two leather moccasins from a boy's burial were made from three main parts: sole, upper portion and cuff around the heel. On one moccasin, a piece of fringed leather is sewn to the upper edge.

9 Arts and Beliefs

Carving bone was a skill that the Beothuk used in making harpoon heads and spear and arrow points. They also used this skill to carve small pendants of bone and antler which they decorated with designs such as triangles, diamonds, ladders or zigzag lines. Each carving looked different from all others. The bone was polished and the patterns filled with red ochre which made the design show up well on the light, shiny bone surface. A hole was carved through at one end, and the pendant was threaded on a thong. Nearly all pendants that are now in museum collections were found in graves, either tied to clothing, arranged as a necklace or wrapped up in packages of about 30 and placed next to the dead person.

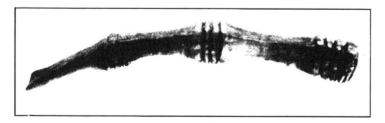

A bone carving in the shape of the bones of a finger, or perhaps of a claw. It was rubbed with ochre, and may have been used as a hunting charm or in the ceremonial honouring of animal spirits.

Because we know little about the beliefs of the Beothuk, we compare their customs and artifacts with those of other tribes. If their lifestyle, habits and artifacts were similar, we guess that their beliefs may have been similar too. This is why we think that the bone pendants were symbols which had to do with Beothuk beliefs that animals, plants and other natural things all had their own spirits. Some of the carvings might represent simple figures of mammals or birds' feet while others look very much like finger joints or the claws of a bear. Most likely the carvings were used as charms or 'amulets' to help in the hunt, to fend off evil spirits, or to give special powers to the wearer. They may also have played an important role in communal ceremonies in honour of animal spirits.

The most respected animal spirit would have been that of the caribou because the Beothuk depended on the caribou for food and clothes in winter. When caribou were killed, the Beothuk followed special rituals and rules or *tabus* so that the caribou spirit would not be offended. Feasts in honour of the caribou spirit centred around eating caribou bone marrow and singing songs. To extract bone marrow, the Beothuk cracked, mashed and boiled a large number of leg bones; to this day, large piles of this bone mash in old mamateek pits, are the tell tale signs of such feasts.

The Beothuk believed that a 'Great Spirit' controlled people and much of nature. They also worshipped the sun and the moon, and feared a sea monster and a kind of Red Indian devil who would punish the wicked. A people who believed in powerful spirits needed a person who knew the spirit world. This man or woman, known as *shaman*, was in charge of ceremonies and offerings in honour of spirits. The shaman's badge of office was a 'medicine bag' containing objects that were thought to hold magic powers. The shaman was also the person to go to for advice about such matters as where to look for animals to hunt, or how to cure a sick person.

For the Beothuk people, death was only a form of sleep. They thought that life would continue in some way, so they buried their dead with great care. The body was wrapped in birch bark or skins and sprinkled with red ochre. It was laid out at full length, or on its side with curled limbs, or propped up in a sitting position. Food, strings of shell beads, weapons and everyday items were placed in the grave so that the spirits of these objects would serve the dead in the other world. Limbs or other parts of animals, packages of red ochre and carved amulets were put in the grave to give spiritual protection. The position and amount of things in the grave probably depended on the importance of the person and whether he or she had been a hunter or a woman or a child.

The Beothuk feared the 'black man' or 'Red Indian devil' called Aich-mud-yim. *Shanawdithit, who drew this picture, said he had a long beard, was short and very thick and dressed in beaver skin. He had been seen at Red Indian Lake.*

The Beothuk often brought their dead to the coast for burial in caves or rock shelters on headlands or islands. If we go by the beliefs of other Indians, the Beothuk believed that a barrier of water kept the spirits of the dead, whom they feared, from returning to the living; these spirits, they thought, could not cross water. About 100 years ago, two boys found the grave of a well-preserved Beothuk boy in a cave on a small island. His fully dressed body was inside an ochre-stained, beaver skin legging with fringes and carved bone pieces and birds' feet tied to it. There were packages of food and ochre and small copies of items for daily use: bows and arrows, canoe images and paddles, bark cups and a carved wooden figure. All these items are now in the Newfoundland Museum.

Only one cemetery was ever discovered inland and this was on the shore of Red Indian Lake. The most notable burial was a hut in which the remains of chief Nonosbawsut, his wife Demasduwit, their child and other persons were laid out. Many grave offerings were placed with them, among them small canoe replicas, decorated birch bark containers, pieces of iron pyrite and carved figures. Remains of other Beothuk were placed in cradles that hung several feet off the ground or were laid in small burial boxes set on the forest floor.

10 *Contacts with White People*

The Vikings were the first white people to discover Newfoundland around 1000 B.P. and their legends tell of encounters with local savages. We cannot be sure whether these natives were Beothuk or Eskimos. Much later, in 1497, John Cabot came to the coast of Newfoundland and brought back to England the news of unexplored northern lands. His report inspired others to follow him, and soon it became known that the Terra Nova or New Land had much useful timber and large fishing grounds. Within a century, fishing fleets from England, Portugal, France and Spain came every summer to Newfoundland to fish. Several of the ships' crews captured natives to bring back to Europe as slaves, or to exhibit as curiosities.

The first recorded European settlement in Newfoundland was founded in 1610 by John Guy in Cupids, Conception Bay. On a voyage of discovery from there into Trinity Bay, Guy met and traded with a group of Beothuk. In exchange for their furs, he gave the Indians knives, axes, needles, scissors and clothes. Guy arranged through signs that they should meet again the next year. The Beothuk came back to the trading place at the proper time but, by chance, another fishing ship arrived. Seeing so many Indians together and believing them to be hostile, the captain fired the ship's cannon into the crowd. The Indians fled, and peaceful trade with the Beothuk was ruined.

In the 1700s many farmers, fishermen and trappers made Newfoundland their new home. They built communities in the sheltered bays and inlets where the Beothuk used to camp in summer. As more settlers came and spread out along the coast, the Beothuk could no longer come to their favourite camp sites on the seashore and were forced to move to places with fewer resources. This meant that they were not able to collect enough food during the summer season to feed themselves and still have enough left for the winter. The Indians began to starve. Probably, Beothuk also died from diseases such as tuberculosis, brought to the island by the white people.

Many settlers and fishermen were afraid of the Red Indians; others wanted to take over their hunting grounds and they were angry when Beothuk stole tools or other useful items from them. This anger caused some of the white people to chase the Indians and kill them, destroying their mamateeks and canoes as they went. Several reports tell of cruel deeds committed against Beothuk men, women and children.

While Indians of other North American tribes became used to the newcomers from Europe and traded and mixed with them, the Beothuk shied away from white people. Bad experiences made them retreat and keep up their traditional way of life as best they could. They defended themselves against the settlers they met, and killed some of them in revenge for their actions. Another threat were the Micmac Indians, who hunted and later settled in Newfoundland and competed with the Beothuk for the territory where the Beothuk had lived for so long.

Although the Beothuk were skilled with their bows and arrows, they could not hold out against enemies with guns, and their tribe became rapidly smaller. Before the white people came to Newfoundland, there may have been between 700 and 1000 Beothuk on the island. By the time the Colonial government started to take an interest in these Indians, only a few hundred of them were left. Several Newfoundland governors tried to protect the Beothuk by ordering all white people and other Indian tribes not to harm or kill them. But the government was too far away to enforce the order, and the killings went on.

In 1768, Captain John Cartwright of the British Navy was sent into Indian country along the Exploits River to find Beothuk and make friends with them. His mission failed for he did not meet a single Indian. However, he made a map of Indian camps that he found and described many of their artifacts. Not until 1811 was a second attempt made to contact the Beothuk. Captain David Buchan with a company of Marines trekked up the Exploits River in mid-winter and surprised Beothuk in their camp at Red Indian Lake. Buchan tried to convince the Indians that he meant well, but the Beothuk were much too frightened to believe him. While Buchan went to fetch presents, they killed the two Marines he had left behind as hostages, and fled.

The last person to try to meet with the Beothuk was William Epps Cormack, a Scot, whose heart went out to the native people. In 1822, guided by a Micmac, he walked right across the island to meet them. His long and tiring journey was not successful because his route did not take him through Beothuk country. In support of the Indians, Cormack founded the 'Beothuck Institution' and set out again to find them in 1827. He searched forests and valleys and climbed hills to look for telltale smoke, but all that he found were abandoned campsites and burials.

We have learned much of what we know about the Beothuk from the reports of settlers and men who went inland in search of the Indians. They described how the Beothuk lived, what their houses, canoes, clothes and weapons looked like, and what animals they hunted and ate. More could have been learned from two Beothuk boys who were captured in 1758 and 1768 and brought up in settler communities to become skilled boatmen. Yet, nobody took the trouble to question them about their beliefs or other parts of their culture. The first list of Beothuk words comes from a nine-year-old Beothuk girl called Oubee, who was captured by fishermen in 1791 and died a few

(Top Left) Three arrowheads from a prehistoric Beothuk campsite. The stem is inserted into a groove on the top end of the arrow shaft and then tied firmly in place. (Left) Game pieces found in Beothuk graves (see also page 44). (Above) a string of flat beads made from shell, pieces of clay pipe stem and birch bark. The beads may have been worn as ornaments or used as counters in games.

(Overleaf) The Beothuk often buried their dead in caves on small islands off the coast of Newfoundland.

The comb (above), the small birch bark dish (top right) and the carved bone pendant (right) were found in Beothuk graves. Indians believed that the spirits of the objects they placed in graves would serve the spirit of the dead person in the afterlife.

(Overleaf) The Beothuk dried fish and meat to preserve it for the long winter months when fresh food was scarce.

years later. Finally, in the early 1800s, information about Beothuk history and their way of life was given by two Beothuk women who lived for a while with white people.

One was Demasduwit, taken prisoner in March 1819, and known as Mary March. Her husband, chief Nonosbawsut, was killed when he came to her aid, and her baby, which was left behind, died soon after. Demasduwit was a tall person with delicate limbs. She had a musical voice, was gentle and intelligent and easily learned the English words she was taught. A list of Beothuk words collected from her has helped relate the Beothuk language to that of other Algonkian tribes. The plan had been to make friends with Demasduwit and then return her to her tribe so that she could tell her people about the good will of her captors. This was not to happen, because Demasduwit died of tuberculosis before she could rejoin her group. A party of Marines carried her body back into Indian country. A portrait of Demasduwit was made during her brief visit to St. John's. It is the only authentic picture of a Beothuk Indian that we have.

In 1823, three sick and starving Beothuk women were found by furriers. One of these, a girl of about twenty, survived. Her name was Shanawdithit and she lived for five years with a settler family who called her Nancy. Shanawdithit was an intelligent and lively person who loved children and had a natural gift for drawing. Sometimes she would be overcome with sadness, and would slip into the woods to talk to her dead mother and sister. Shanawdithit was afraid to return to her tribe, fearing that she would not be forgiven for having lived with white people.

Shanawdithit's sketch of the house in St. John's where she stayed. The small drawing underneath was made by Cormack to show the actual appearance of the house.

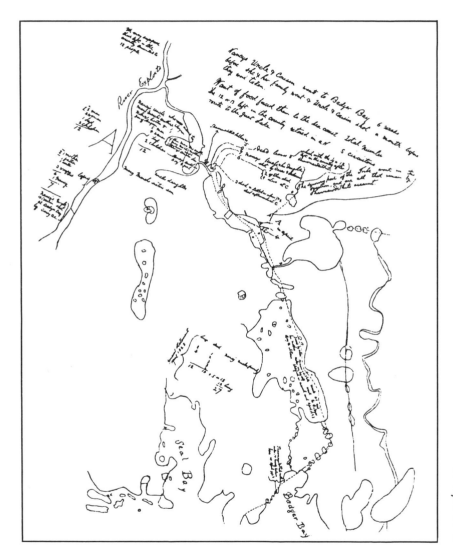

When Cormack came back from his second excursion in search of Beothuk in 1827, people realized that Shanawdithit might be one of the last of the Beothuk, so Cormack took her to St. John's. It was to him that she talked about the way of life and history of the Beothuk people and dictated many words of the Beothuk language. Shanawdithit also made a series of drawings. They showed earlier meetings between the Indians and white people, mamateeks, food, tools, the emblems of chiefs, the Red Indian devil and a dancing woman, but her explanations, as written down by Cormack, cannot be fully understood. In 1829, Shanawdithit died in St. John's from tuberculosis and, after her death, no more Beothuk were found in Newfoundland. A few survivors may have joined other Indians in Labrador, but as an independent tribe the Beothuk had vanished.

This map, drawn by Shanawdithit, shows the country inland from Seal and Badger Bays where the surviving Beothuk (most her own and Demasduwit's family) camped. The map also shows the route Shanawdithit, her mother and sister took and where they were found by furriers who brought them to Exploits Island.

42

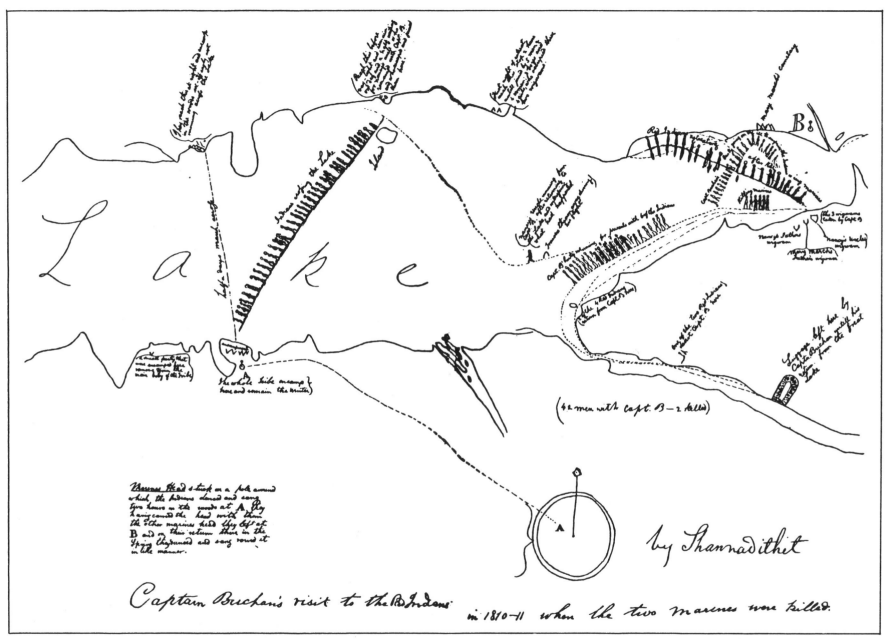

Shanawdithit's story of Captain Buchan's surprise visit to their camp at Red Indian Lake. It shows the arrival of Buchan and his Marines at the three mamateeks (right); Buchan returning with four of the Indians to his last campsite; the killing of the two Marines; the flight of the Indians to a remote part of the country. A and B are the places where the Marines' heads were stuck on poles for a celebration.

43

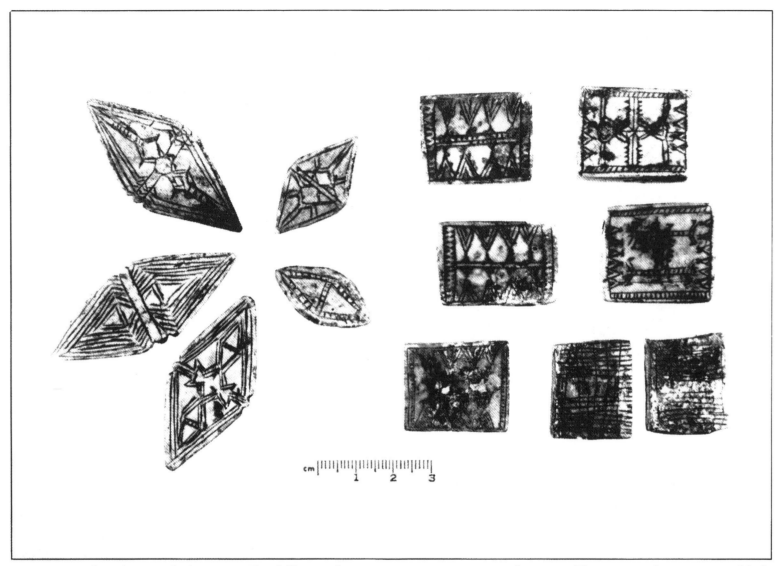

Game pieces found in Beothuk graves. The different shapes may represent men and women. The engraved patterns are likely to have had a symbolic meaning, perhaps representing the people and their ancestors, or the earth and the netherworld.

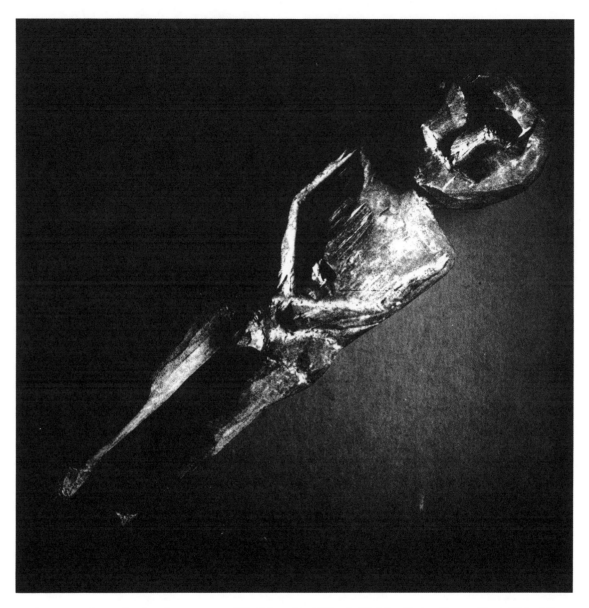

Male image from the boy's grave on Big Island in Pilley's Tickle, Notre Dame Bay. This 19cm high figure is carved from wood and rubbed with red ochre. The remains of the boy were covered with a canopy of birch bark, taken from an old canoe; rocks and gravel were piled on top.